CONSTITUTIONS

CONSTITUTIONS

JOHN OF THORESBY

Copyright 2025 by Dalcassian Press

All rights reserved. No part of this book may be reproduced in any manner whatsoever without written permission except in the case of brief quotations embodied in critical articles and reviews.

No part of this publication may be reproduced, distributed, or transmitted in any form or by any means, including photocopying, recording, or other electronic or mechanical methods, without the prior written permission of the publisher, except in the case of brief quotations embodied in critical reviews and certain other non-commercial uses permitted by copyright law. For permission request, write to Dalcassian Press at admin@thescriptoriumproject.com

Translator: Curtin, D.P. (1985-)

ISBN: 979-8-3485-4112-5 (Paperback)
ISBN: 979-8-3485-4111-8 (eBook)
Library of Congress Control Number:

Printed by Ingram Content Group, 1 Ingram Blvd, La Vergne, Tennessee
First Printing 2025, Dalcassian Press, Wilmington, DE

This work is part of a series produced in association with the Scriptorium Project and its community of scholars and translators.
Please visit our website at: www.thescriptoriumproject.com

CONSTITIONS OF JOHN THORESBY

Archbishop of York, published in the year of our Lord 1367

John, by divine permission Archbishop of York, Primate of England, etc. We execute the duty of our office as we prudently ordain those things that promote the decorum of the church and regard the salvation of souls, as well as restrain and repress the excesses and abuses of subordinates. Therefore, wishing to counter certain errors and abuses that we know have gained a foothold in the church:

That on sacred days, no markets, fairs, or games are to be held.
Firstly, following the example of Christ, who wished to call His holy church, His own house, not a house of trade, but a house of prayer; not wanting the dealings, in which anyone strives, as it is commonly said, to deceive his neighbor, to be exercised there; He cast out those selling and buying from the temple, lest they make His house a den of fraud and a den of thieves; we firmly prohibit that anyone hold a market or trade in our diocesan churches, or their porches, or cemeteries, or other sacred places on Sundays and feast days, nor exercise any trade therein, nor hold any secular courts in the same, nor shall there be wrestling, fighting, or games there, which may provide cause or occasion for sin, dissension, hatred, or fighting; but let every Catholic reverently approach there to pray, and humbly implore the forgiveness of sins.

Regarding dishonorable games on the vigils of saints and the funerals of the deceased, they are prohibited.

And because it often happens that certain individuals gather in churches on the vigils of saints, they should devote themselves there to divine services, or in the funerals of the deceased, praying for the souls of the departed, who, in contrast, frequently engage in harmful games, vanities, and sometimes worse things, gravely offending God and the saints (whom they pretend to venerate), and in the funerals of the deceased, turning the house of mourning and prayer into a house of laughter and excess, which is very serious for the danger of their souls; we strictly prohibit that anyone coming to such vigils and funerals, especially in churches, should engage in such games or indecencies, or do anything that leads to error or sin in any way; but let anyone coming strive to do so humbly and devoutly, for which such vigils and funerals were ordained: we firmly enjoin all and singular rectors, vicars, and others holding any ecclesiastical benefices, to canonically prohibit and restrain such insolences and excesses in their churches, cemeteries, and places dedicated to God, under the penalty of twenty solidi, which shall be imposed on the same rectors, vicars, and beneficed individuals, whenever and wherever, concerning the execution of such constitution, if it should be found that they have committed negligence in the premises or any of the premises, we wish them to be applied to the fabric of our cathedral church; and the perpetrators of such excesses shall be entirely interdicted from the church, which they sought to pollute, and they shall not have access to hear divine services and to receive ecclesiastical sacraments therein until they have made satisfaction for the offenses committed.

Innovations of synodal constitutions.

Furthermore, since in cases where sufficient provision is made by previously published laws, there is no need for the promulgation of new constitutions or laws; we, having more closely reviewed the synodal statutes promulgated in the times of our predecessors, find in them the same by the constitution, which begins thus: "Furthermore, the stipends of priests for one year are to be assessed at five marks; however, in wealthier churches, we wish to provide more abundantly according to their resources." And, by the constitution (of good memory) of William de la Zouche, our immediate predecessor, concerning the salaries of stipendiary priests, and concerning chaplains serving the care of souls, to be well and reasonably provided for other ministers, we renew those ordinances or constitutions abundantly; strictly commanding that they be observed inviolably according to their force, form, and effect, and that the synodal constitutions be regarded as true in the future, of which the renewals are such.

Of the stipends of parish chaplains and others.
William, by divine permission, etc., believes that he should exercise the pastoral office due at that time, while diligently aiming for the benefit of our subjects and their peace. Indeed, considering recently and more attentively the difficulties and excesses that stipendiary chaplains have caused regarding the agreement and collection of their annual stipends, due to the lack and rarity of such chaplains, and those existing these days, which have hindered and continue to hinder until now, and wishing to diligently restrain and moderate such difficulties and excesses as much as we can with God's help, in this case, so that the benefit of our subjects may be provided for, we have deemed it necessary, with the counsel of legal experts assisting us, and after having had fuller deliberation, to ordain and also to establish that all and each chaplain, both those ordained in the past and those to be ordained in the future, shall be content with the stipends inscribed below, under the penalty noted below; namely, that no chaplain, even if he should be a parish chaplain, shall receive in any way beyond the sum of six marks in counted money, or its equivalent in other things, for his annual stipend from anyone; which stipends, considering the considerations, especially given the rarity of chaplains during such time, are deemed sufficient. We prohibit all and each of such chaplains, whether ordained or to be ordained, that no one among them, under the penalty of suspension from the celebration of divine ser-

vices for one year, shall receive in any way in money or value beyond the sum of six marks as stated for his annual stipend; and if anyone does so, we decree that he shall incur the said suspension by that very act.

To all rectors and each ecclesiastical authority.

To the prelates, vicars, and any other persons of the church, chapels, chantries, oratories, hospitals, or any ecclesiastical benefices within our diocese, we similarly prohibit, under the virtue of holy obedience and under the penalty of forty solidi of our alms, that in their churches, chapels, chantries, hospitals, or other such benefices, they permit any stipendiary chaplain to celebrate divine services, unless it concerns an annual stipend of six marks. To all and each of these, under the virtue of holy obedience and under a similar penalty, we also prohibit that any such stipendiary chaplain be henceforth admitted to celebrate anniversary masses or special services in churches, chapels, chantries, oratories, hospitals, or any ecclesiastical places of our said diocese, or be permitted to do so, before provision has first been made for parochial chaplains of such places regarding the stipulated stipends. And, lest our ordinances, prohibitions, and statutes of this kind lack effect and vigor through non-use or abuse, we will and ordain in these writings that in each synod of Easter and St. Michael, celebrated in our church of York, and at other opportune times, a diligent and exact inquiry be made and held every year; to the effect that those who do not observe the aforementioned shall be canonically punished with the aforementioned penalties and others, as it may seem expedient. However, by these present ordinances and statutes, which we issue and make public due to the current rarity of chaplains, we do not intend nor wish to derogate from the synodal constitution previously issued and promulgated regarding the receipt of stipends of such hired chaplains.

Of mothers and nurses of infants, and their caution.

Also, since it often happens that mothers and nurses of infants, whom they nurture, carelessly place them beside themselves in their beds, a frequent and very painful oppression or suffocation of such infants arises, and thus the occasion of death proceeds from where consolation of life was hoped for; we forbid that fathers, or mothers, nurses, or any others who have custody of infants, place them in their own beds or rooms; but rather that they place them in cradles or other safe places, where the fear of such suffocation does not arise, or have them placed there, or while ministering milk to the infants, take sleep in any way over their cradles.

Concerning freely receiving, carrying away, and taking away tithes.

Also, although God and Lord, whose is the earth and the fullness thereof, graciously arranging all things, has granted to His people the land to be cultivated and governed, reserving the tithes of their fruits and works for the priests and Levites, to minister in the churches, in the strength of the Lord's precept. By the virtue of the divine reservation, the rectors of churches, and the persons of the ecclesiastical church freely receive the tithes of the crops and other things existing within the parishes entrusted to them, and they have freely and lawfully received them from the same places, from which and by which the lordly lords lack nine parts of such crops, and they have caused them to be received by others, and the said rectors and ecclesiastical persons have been in possession, or quasi liberty of such, for a time of which there is no memory of the contrary, continuously, peacefully, and quietly. However, certain degenerate and ungrateful sons of the holy mother church, weighing the heavenly grace granted to them regarding the nine parts less duly, strive through exquisite malice and unlawful impediments to hinder ecclesiastical persons, ministers of Christ, in the free reception of the tithe parts in various ways; for some seek to freely receive the tithes themselves and to be taken away by the paths and journeys by which they have been accustomed to be carried, and they maliciously compel them to be carried through long and harmful routes; some also do not allow the crops exposed and marked for the tithe to be carried away from their lands, as long as anything of the grains remains in them, but they knowingly and fraudulently tolerate the tithes to be gathered and consumed by their and others' beasts; and they do not allow the rectors to arrange for such tithes, to the offense of divine majesty, a notorious violation of ecclesiastical liberty, and a not insignificant damage and burden to the said rectors and ecclesiastical persons, and a pernicious example to others. Therefore, wishing, as we are bound by the duty of our office, to provide healthily against such malice and injuries, unjustly inflicted in contempt of God and His church; by the authority of this present constitution, we firmly prohibit that anyone, of whatever state, condition, or degree, the rectors of churches, or other ecclesiastical persons, or their servants and ministers, shall hinder or disturb, to the extent that they may not freely and integrally receive and apprehend the tithes of crops, hay, and other things pertaining to them and their churches, wherever and whenever they may occur, without the consumption of animals and any other voluntary and harmful diminution of the same; and that they may not impede or disturb their ability to carry them away through all places, by which the nine parts are carried and have been accustomed to be carried, and to carry them away more conveniently by vehicles, and to dispose of them at their will, under the penalty of major excommunication against all and singular contraveners, which we wish them to incur by that very act.

Regarding fraudulent alienations condemned.
Indeed, the most terrible corruption, invented through the deceit and cunning of certain individuals, has taken root in our dioceses and province, such that certain ecclesiastical men, prelates, and others included in the clerical order, and some laymen, while considering the danger of death approaching, presume to donate or in any way alienate all their goods, or some of them, so that not only the church but also the king and others creditors, to whom such alienators, while they

lived, were bound by various causes and effectively obligated, are excluded from actions and prosecutions, and wives and children are irreparably defrauded of their share of goods, whether by custom or by law. Some even, assisting such sick individuals in extremis, maliciously persuade such alienations to take place, and rashly induce them, and wickedly and cunningly divert them from their free will to testify, from which the usual and legitimate making of a testament mostly passes into abuse of churches, and the rights and prosecutions of others are unduly or maliciously derogated. Therefore, by prudent deliberation of the provincial council, held in the chapter house of our church of Ebora, it was prohibited under the precept that such alienations or donations be made in the future under any color or pretext. And because, as experience teaches, a general prohibition does not revoke those given over to malice from executing an evil purpose, unless they are compelled by the fear of a special penalty, we, by the authority of this synod, prohibit all and singular from giving counsel, assistance, or favor in our diocese regarding such donations or alienations. Moreover, those who make such donations and alienate their goods in our aforementioned diocese shall be deprived of ecclesiastical burial due to the gravity of their excesses, but a pact of fraud or malice is proven to have intervened in this case, whenever someone alienates all their goods, under whatever title, as previously mentioned, among the living; or in such an immense quantity that the church, the king, creditors, the wife, and children cannot be satisfied from the residue, as justice and custom would require, if such an alienation had not been made in this manner.

Regarding the behavior, demeanor, and honesty of clerics.

Furthermore, since all ostentation of bodily lasciviousness must be entirely alien to the sacred order, it is provided by the sacred canons and holy fathers that it be prohibited under severe penalties and censures, that ecclesiastical men in sacred orders, especially priests, whose behavior should serve as an example and model of living for the laity, should not wear garments that are excessively short, which would be ridiculous or notorious; nor should they seek glory or adornment in their footwear, but rather strive to please God and men in the state of mind and demeanor of the body, so that through the decency of external attire, the honesty of internal morals may be shown; yet nothing should be apparent in them that offends the eyes or sight of those looking on: for according to the scriptures, the disarray of the body indicates the quality of the mind, and from an indecent appearance, the one who bears it appears vile, and the hearts of the viewers are scandalized by the ease of judgment. Some, however, as evident from the facts and reputation, and clerics established in sacred orders and priesthood, forgetful of their own dignity, and rashly pursuing the honor of their clerical office and order, have publicly worn garments that are shamefully cut. Fathers, with regard to the medium of their thighs, a base kind that does not in any way touch upon decency and the honesty of their clerical priestly order, for the sake of boasting and the display of their bodies, and the dissolution of morals, without reasonable cause and honest justification, do not cease to publicly and commonly engage in this daily, to the peril of their souls, a grave scandal to the clerical order and the Church of God, and a pernicious example for other faithful of Christ. Therefore, wishing to address such insolences and the dangers to souls, this sacred provincial council has decreed and established that any penalties, whether centuries or otherwise, in such constitutions, canons, and statutes shall be executed against such offenders in any manner whatsoever, etc.

That matrimonial and divorce cases be entrusted to experts and dealt with publicly, and decided.

Furthermore, because some archdeacons, deans, abbots, and other ecclesiastical men, claiming to have ecclesiastical jurisdiction and knowledge of matrimonial cases, do not hesitate to entrust matrimonial cases, which should be dealt with more diligently and resolved sooner by discrete judges, to simple and unskilled persons for examination and resolution, in modern times indistinctly, against the canonical sanctions and the institutions of the holy fathers; and such insufficient persons, and sometimes laymen, presume to appoint officials, commissioners, or custodians with the power to be adjudicated in such matrimonial cases, putting their own souls in grave danger and causing a more pernicious prejudice to the republic; and those officials or custodians, as previously mentioned, appointed, also commit their duties improperly to other insufficient and unskilled persons, sometimes involving a notable amount of money, to adjudicate among certain persons on such matrimonial cases and to resolve them. Officials, as guardians of the property, through themselves and their insufficient commissioners, as previously stated, in and about matrimonial and divorce cases, not only to know, but also to issue unjust sentences and multiply indiscreetly, which they presume to deliver as definitive, and to promulgate more dangerously; from which we have found not only serious scandals but also many daily dangers to souls. We, Johannes, archbishop, by the counsel of our suffragans and our clergy, gathered in our provincial council, wishing to close the way to such scandals, and as much as we can with God's help, to avert dangers, adhering to the footsteps of the holy fathers and sacred canons, do hereby prohibit and firmly forbid all and singular archdeacons, deans, abbots, prelates, and other ecclesiastical men of whatever our cities, dioceses, and province of York holding ecclesiastical jurisdiction, and their officials, and those appointed or to be appointed as guardians of such spiritual matters. The aforementioned archdeacons, deans, abbots, prelates, or others do not appoint any officials, at the custody of the officials, with authority over matrimonial causes or divorces, regarding the recognition, to appoint or designate, or to delegate their powers in this matter; or those officials, or custodians, to adjudicate on such matters, to some or anyone, less qualified, or other than suitable, prudent, or trustworthy men, having legal expertise, or at least competent practice in judging such matters, may commit, or any of them may delegate their powers in any way, or by themselves elsewhere than in the chapters to be celebrated by them, to resolve or decide such cases; but publicly in the same chapters they shall pronounce what they deem to be established, or under penalty regarding the archdeacons, deans, abbots, provosts, and other ecclesiastical men, however they may be named, claiming jurisdiction or authority for themselves, such officials, or custodians to be appointed, suspension from office, and regarding such officials delegating their powers in the aforementioned insufficient matters, and regarding such insufficient commissioners, and those insufficiently and knowingly admitted, and adjudicating on such matters, the sentence of greater excommunication; which penalties we wish to be incurred by all and each who shall have presumed against this present constitution, or statute, knowingly, or through affected ignorance, and gross or supine, and have not observed it with effect, as distinguished and more fully declared above, by the very fact.

Of clandestinely contracted marriages.

Moreover, although clandestine marriages, from which the dangers of souls and bodies often arise most grievously, are condemned by sacred canons, as being harmful to those contracting them and to the republic, and are to be done under severe penalties, yet some, cunningly devising to contract illicit marriages secretly, so that their evil deeds may not be exposed, flee from the light, seeking darkness, without the proper and lawful publication of banns, rashly disregarding the fear of God and the prohibition of the laws, cause such marriages to be solemnized by chaplains, not without grave scandal to the Church and dangers to souls, procuring damnably day by day and presuming upon the penalties laid out and promulgated against those contracting, celebrating, and being present at such marriages, showing no fear. Therefore, we, the archbishop, with the consent of our suffragans and the aforementioned clergy, wishing to repress the audacity and temerity of such chaplains and persons contracting in this manner, by the accumulation of penalties; prohibit under the penalty of major excommunication, as noted above, which all of our cities, dioceses, and provinces aforementioned, who shall presume to contravene this our constitution, shall incur by that very fact: and that no secular or regular priest of whatever condition shall clandestinely contract marriage. The definitive celebration, or the presence of those preferring it, if ever a marriage is to be solemnized between any persons in churches or chapels of their respective parishes, let the publication of banns take place, and let the edict be publicly proposed for three solemn days, within the competent term set forth, so that within that term, whoever wishes and is able may oppose any impediment, and the priest shall nonetheless investigate whether any impediment exists, or whether anyone appears to claim in this matter, or in any way contradicts: if it appears that there is a contradiction against the union to be contracted, or a probable conjecture of a contract, it shall not be celebrated, but expressly prohibited, until what should be done regarding it has been lawfully declared by a competent judge in this matter, or otherwise by the license of a superior ordinary, when those wishing to contract have been dispensed regarding the intervals of time and the publication of banns; we reserve the absolution of all those who may fall into such penalties, except in the article of death, concerning such impediments in our cities, dioceses, and the persons thereof, and our suffragans in their cities and dioceses, or our superiors specifically. We declare sentences or pronouncements in any matrimonial or divorce cases, promulgated in any way against the tenor of this constitution, to be null and void; and we entirely vacate them of their own force, so that no sentence issued by such persons shall have the name or effect of a sentence. Always saving the constitutions (of good memory) of Otto, formerly legate of the apostolic see in England, concerning the provisionally promulgated cognition of such matters, and any other constitutions, canons, and statutes issued concerning the above, which we do not intend to derogate from in any way, but which we wish and desire to be observed.

That these present constitutions be published.

And, lest our ordinances, constitutions, and inhibitions regarding all the above lack effect (which may it not be) and vigor due to nonuse or abuse; we wish, order, and command all our subjects, under the aforementioned penalty, to mandate in these writings that in every chapter to be celebrated in every deanery, in cities, and other places, and at appropriate times, all and singular of the above be read and solemnly published by the deans; and that every year an inquiry be made and held diligently and accurately regarding the above; to the effect that those who do not observe the above may be canonically punished with the aforementioned penalties and others, as shall seem expedient.

That rectors and vicars have copies of the same.

And, lest rectors, vicars, and other subjects of ours from the clergy and people may claim ignorance of the above in the future; we enjoin all and singular rectors and vicars, under the virtue of obedience, and under the aforementioned penalties, that they, and each of them, have true copies of the aforementioned provisions, within two months from the time of their first publication made to them, they shall have and receive; and they shall observe all and singular in all and singular articles, and publicly announce and explain them to their parishioners and subjects on every Sunday, as they wish to avoid the penalty of canonical retribution. In witness of all these provisions, we have caused our seal to be affixed. Given at Thorp near York, concerning the confirmation, on the penultimate day of the month of September, in the year of our Lord 1267, and of our consecration the fifteenth.

Modified statute in the provincial council.

It should be noted that this statute was later modified and restricted in another provincial council, so that excommunication does not occur except in certain cases; namely, that those contracting, knowing of a legitimate impediment, even if nothing is objected in the publication of banns, are excommunicated. Likewise, those contracting without the publication of banns, solemnizing marriage, are excommunicated, as is also the presbyter solemnizing. Likewise, where those contracting solemnize marriage, where an impediment is objected to in the publication of banns, without having discussed the impediment beforehand, are excommunicated. Likewise, compelling a chaplain through fear to solemnize clandestine marriage. Likewise, a chaplain, not publishing banns for three solemn days, and solemnizing marriage, or afterwards an impediment appears. Likewise, those contracting against the interdict of the church, in such cases are excommunicated by the very fact, and not in others.

Reserved cases to the Archbishop of York.

And because both rectors, vicars, and presbyters admit their parishioners to confession indiscriminately, not distinguishing between grave crimes and light ones; although in some cases irregularity is incurred, in others, although irregularity is not contracted, absolution is nevertheless reserved to the Apostolic See, and sometimes it is permitted or granted to us to give absolution in the same. Greater crimes, which we and our penitentiary retain, we shall make clear in a brief, God willing, so that in cases where absolution pertains to us, we absolve confessors, but in others we send them to the Apostolic See for absolution, as is proper to be obtained.

The first case is with one who sins against faith.

The second is in one who sins against nature; and especially with beasts. The third case is in one who commits homicide. The fourth is in one who sins against God, or any of the saints, publicly blaspheming. The fifth is in one who sins against the church, violently breaking, or violating ecclesiastical immunities or liberties. The sixth is committing incest. The seventh is committing notorious adultery. The eighth is by committing perjury and by holding a false testimony. The ninth is in committing simony. The tenth is in committing fortilege. The eleventh is in those who make conspiracies and plots against their superiors. The twelfth is in committing arson. The thirteenth is in selling against a lawful and honest vow. The fourteenth is in parents who oppress their children. The fifteenth is in those who corrupt sanctimoniales. The sixteenth is in one who lays violent hands on a cleric or any religious person, or who, when able, does not protect them from violent hands; or who detains an enemy cleric, even if not laying hands on them, by perhaps placing them in custody or enclosing them within some house. The seventeenth is in one who, by himself or through another, has forged letters of some lord, or has supported such forgers, or defended them. The eighteenth is in one who has had such forged letters from another and has knowingly used them. The nineteenth is in archdeacons, deans, parish priests, prelates, cantors, and other clerics having personatus, as well as in priests hearing law or physical cases, unless they desist within a period of two months. The twentieth is in one who participates in a crime, due to his crime, with an excommunicated person. The twenty-first is in one who voluntarily and knowingly participates with an excommunicated person in divine offices. The twenty-second is in those who impose exactions or undue burdens on churches, priests, and their possessions, unless they desist when warned. The twenty-third is in usurers public and in those who receive offerings from them, or admit them to ecclesiastical burial. The twenty-fourth is in one who celebrates or otherwise officiates in his order, excommunicated with a greater excommunication, or suspended, or interdicted by man. The twenty-fifth is in a cleric who approaches the judgment of a secular prince, having contempt for the ecclesiastical judge. The twenty-sixth is in a cleric who has contracted bigamy. The twenty-seventh is in a non-ordained cleric ministering. The twenty-eighth is in a cleric promoted to orders by fault. The twenty-ninth is in one who has secretly received orders. The thirtieth is if someone has made himself to be ordained again in the same order. The thirty-first is in one who has made himself to be baptized again. The thirty-second is if he has adhered to heretics for the subversion of faith, and has made himself to be baptized or ordained by them in contempt of the church. The thirty-third is in one ordained outside the four times, or otherwise illicitly, and ministering before obtaining dispensation. The thirty-fourth case is in one who has been suspended from divine offices by canon, and thus suspended while celebrating the divine. In the case where the supreme pontiff reserves dispensation for himself, in the case of that canon which begins: "Of or from:" and 2. namely in the sixth book. For indeed." And in the case of the canon which begins thus: "When medicinal:" both of which are from the council of Lyons, the thirty-fifth is in one who has received orders in the sentence of excommunication. The thirty-sixth is in those who take something from the houses, manors, or granaries, or other places of archbishops, bishops, or other ecclesiastical persons, against their will, or who take away, consume, or wrongfully handle something. The thirty-seventh is, and the last in those who have publicly committed heinous crimes, for which the whole city, town, village, or country is stirred, for which public penance must be imposed. Therefore, in these excesses, and others which are counted among the greater ones, we wish that the delinquent be sent to us or our penitentiary, except in the article of death. However, we command that letters be granted freely to the penitent, and, that it may be clear, what kind of penance it has been, and for what crime it has been imposed, the penitent shall bear letters from the penitentiary to the sender, who shall not remit the penance imposed by the penitentiary; but neither shall he presume to change it in any way under the penalty of suspension from office, which he himself incurs by the very act, if he does otherwise, until he has deserved to obtain our grace.

This work was produced in association with:

www.ingramcontent.com/pod-product-compliance
Lightning Source LLC
LaVergne TN
LVHW061050070526
838201LV00074B/5245